Sales

A Beginners Guide to Master Simple
Sales Techniques and Increase Sales
(sales, best tips, sales tools, sales strategy,
close the deal, business development,
influence people, cold calling)

DANIEL R.COVEY

CONTENTS

I think next books will also be interesting for you.

How to Organize Your Life

Leadership and Coaching

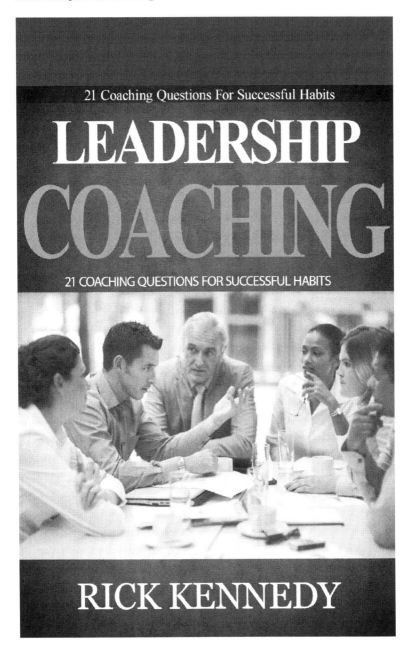

Introduction

The foundation of every business is sales, for without selling anything, businesses would not survive the tough markets that they are in today. It is important then, for businesses and individuals alike, to then learn all of the necessary skills to be successful in sales and then keep learning as the market constantly changes and evolves.

However, the sales industry is much more than being about sales – it must be about your customers, and more specifically, the needs of your customers. In order to understand these needs you must be asking questions to identify these needs – for if you do not ask what it is that your customer actually wants, then how will you possibly know what it is that they want?

For that reason, to be successful in the sales industry, you must change your focus from making sales to making relationships. Businesses are built on repeat business and customers buy things from the people that they trust, so this should be your focus.

This book is a beginners guide to mastering simple sales techniques in order to increase sales, and will cover all of the necessary factors which are required in order to achieve this. You will learn everything from how to develop relationships, to overcoming customer objections, and the latest tools and sales strategies of which you can use on your journey to becoming a successful salesperson.

Chapter 1 – What is Sales?

In the recent movie *The Wolf of Wall Street*, directed my Martin Scorsese, there is a scene in which the protagonist, Jordan Belfort (played by Leonardo DiCaprio), asks his friends to "Sell me this pen". Most of his friends start by saying how appealing or attractive this pen would be to Jordan, thinking that the key to sales is to pitch to the customer the products features and attributes. However, one of the friends, Brad, immediately grabs then pen and asks Jordan to write something down for him. Jordan replies that he does not have a pen to do so, and thus the sale is made. This is the definition of sales. The character Brad realizes what Jordan is asking him to do. He is not really asking his friends to sell him the pen, rather he is asking them to realize that sales is all about the needs of the buyer. People are not going to buy what they do not need or what they do not want – they will only buy what is of immediate value to them.

There is a saying which says "No one buys what you sell, they only buy what is of value to them". This basically means that you should not be selling the marketing of a product (its features and benefits), but rather you should be selling your product as an actual solution to fill your customers needs. In the *Wolf of Wall Street* example above, Brad has recognized that Jordan does not have a pen, so he is able to fill the need of selling Jordan a pen the moment he actually needs a pen. The customer has gone from not valuing the pen one moment (by listening to all the various features and benefits of the pen), to valuing it strong enough the next moment that he needs to buy it. If you are able to recognize the needs of your customers as well as this example, you will go very far as a professional salesperson.

HOW DOES SALES DIFFER FROM MARKETING?

The most effective salespeople in business today don't want their customers to buy *from* them, but rather they want their customers to build a relationship *with* them. The key to a successful sales business is repeat business. This relationship should ultimately be built on trust, and even though there are some very crafty salespeople out there who can get people to even buy what they do not need, this dishonesty and greed will eventually bring any business down, as customers only buy from people of whom they trust. Just as much as you are trying to build customers for life, if they find out that you have been lying to them, you will lose those customers for life.

The biggest difference between sales and marketing is that although both lead to sales, marketing tends to be more about features and benefits to a wide audience at once, whereas sales is generally a personalized and tailored one-on-one experience. Marketing tells stories to the customer, and sales is where those stories become real for the customer. Marketing also looks after the brands reputation, whereas sales looks after individuals. As you can see, although marketing and sales seem very similar in nature, and essentially work towards the same goal in the business world, they are defined in two completely different ways. So make sure that you know the difference when applying them to your business or personal career.

WHAT TRAITS DO SUCCESSFUL SALESPEOPLE HAVE?

Every person who is in the sales business will approach their sales methods in different ways. For example, one sales person might offer each of his customers a coffee, whereas another salesperson might simply wear a suit and tie and be neat and presentable at all times. However, apart from their methods, every successful salesperson shares five traits: discipline, tenacity, implementation, focus and desire. Some salespeople might have more focus than desire, and some salespeople might have more tenacity than implementation, but what is important here is understanding that if you are able to develop each of these five traits, then you will become a very successful salesperson.

DISCIPLINE

The definition of discipline is to create daily habits that you stick to doing and achieving every single day. Discipline and habits can be considered the same thing, for as we discipline ourselves to do things, over time these will become habits that we will not even have to think about doing for them to get done. When was the last time that you had to think about brushing your teeth before bed? Develop this level of discipline in relation to the sales tools needed to succeed, and you will surely succeed.

TENACITY

Tenacity means the quality or fact of being able to grip something firmly or relentlessly. In other words, an all-or-nothing attitude. To apply this to a salesperson, to be successful you must give your customers and business your complete attention at all times. Remember, that at the root of any sales process is the exchange of or potential of money, so don't let an opportunity pass you just because you couldn't be bothered to remain engaged or give the potential sale 100% of your attention.

IMPLEMENTATION

Implementation is probably one of the most important traits that a successful salesperson can have. To implement something basically means to put into action what you have learned. In other words, you should implement or put into practice the key tools and strategies that you are learning whilst reading this book. Also make it a good habit to not give yourself the excuse that you are not smart enough to do something, or don't have the right tools to succeed – just remember that it is up to you to learn new things and then to apply those in your life, business and career.

FOCUS

Focus means to hold your attention strongly and completely on a goal that you wish strongly to achieve. It also means not allowing distractions to get in the way between you and those goals, or other people distracting you by telling you that you are not good enough or not better than them. It will be good practice for you to practice the art of concentration so that you can create for yourself powerful focus for anything that you want in life. See if you can count to 100 without thinking about anything else other than counting. If you start thinking about other things or forget what number you were up to, start from one again until you can reach 100 without being distracted. This is the level of focus that you should learn to cultivate.

DESIRE

You must want your goals and success as much as you want to breathe after holding your breath for a minute. Desire is the ultimate trait out of these five, because if you don't want something then you are not going to do anything about trying to reach it. Just make sure that you remain realistic and understand that success does not happen overnight. It will take some time, so work on developing these five traits every day, and before you know it, you will be a very successful salesperson.

Chapter 2 – How to Close the Sale

Once we have identified what the customer needs, as explained at the start of Chapter One, we can then work on actually making the sale by giving the customer what they need. However, sometimes it takes a little bit more work than asking the question "do you want to buy this product", because you may find that the customer will feel pressured and say no. It's funny, because even though we have exactly what the customer wants, there is something deep within the human psyche that still wants to push back and reject any offer of salvation. As a guide, instead of asking for the purchase, why not try asking the following question instead.

"If I gave you the product at this low price, would there be any reason why you would not want to buy it today?"

This suddenly makes the customer realize that they are going to have to say more than "yes" or "no", although if the customer does say "no" then you have effectively made the sale. However, if the customer says that there is a reason why they do not want to product today, then you can ask further questions to find out what is holding them back. Perhaps the price is out of their budget range, or maybe they wanted a different color or style of the product that you are offering them.

Asking quality questions is the most important first step of the sales process. If we ask customers what they want, we will know what they want. Sometimes we may have to ask different questions to get the need out of them, such as *"What can I do today that is going to help you the most?"*, because if we just ask for the sale without understanding exactly what it is that the customer wants, then they will see right through us. Remember that successful salespeople and sales businesses are built on trust and relationships. If we see the customer's merely as dollar signs rather than human beings with feelings and needs, then we will not go very far at all in the sales business. This is why you should always be having conversations with your customers instead of merely asking them straight away if they want to buy your products.

Chapter 3 – Sales Tools

When most people think about the tools that they can use in their sales business or sales career, they immediately think about CRM (Customer Relationship Management) software such as SalesForce.com, or networking social media websites such as LinkedIn.

It is important to understand that humans have been using

tools for thousands of years, from the prehistoric to the modern man – so too have the tools of technology have evolved and are now today quite incredibly advanced. Just think about what we can do on our phones today that we could not do even 5 years ago.

The same rule applies to the tools within the sales industry. Unlike the sales professionals of days gone past, sales are no longer done exclusively with a telephone directory and a headset. Here are nine sales tools that you should consider should you want to be ahead of your competition.

YESWARE and SIGNALS

Most communication between businesses and customers these days is done through email. But we all should know the pain of sending an email and waiting for a reply, always asking ourselves "have they even opened the email yet?". Luckily both of these tools can help. Yesware and Signals work by alerting us as soon as our customer opens their email and reads it. This provides the perfect opportunity to call them. Imagine how highly they will think of you if they have just finished reading your prospectus and then you call.

BOOMERANG

There are certain times of the day that are considered to be the best time to send somebody an email that they will actually read – the earlier the better as the old saying goes. People are more likely to read a new email whilst they are reading their inbox, which normally occurs in the period between 8:30 and 9am. However, what if you are scheduled for a meeting then? Luckily with this tool, you can schedule certain times for emails to be sent that you have pre-written, making sure that you never miss out on the golden hour of opportunity.

LINKEDIN and other SOCIAL MEDIA

Most people regard LinkedIn as only a social media platform to look for work or employment. However, this is not the case anymore, and innovative sales professionals at the head of the game have realized that LinkedIn and other social media platforms (such as Facebook, Twitter and Google+) are perfect for finding new prospects to sell to. Join groups within your target market, and start doing your research to dish out those sales.

GOOGLE ALERTS

Google Alerts is a very powerful tool, in that it does all of your social media browsing for you. No longer do you have to go through each of the pages of your social media platforms to read the latest updates from your friends, groups and followers. This tool will alert you each time one of these people posts a new update, meaning that you will have access to the latest news, even before your competition if they do not have this tool. This is how you stay ahead in the sales business.

RAPPORTIVE

Rapportive is a free sales tool which will link together your LinkedIn and Gmail accounts, so that when we are emailing our client or prospect, we will see a brief summary of their LinkedIn account on the side so not only do we know who we are emailing (especially if emailing a lot of people every day), but also so that we are able to build strong rapport and relationships with these people by commenting on their latest update for example. Remember that relationships are key to a successful sales business or career.

SALES LOFT

Sales Loft will save you hundreds of hours of work by importing all of your social media contacts into one database, complete with email addresses and phone numbers, which then can be used as a contact directory, or even for your next marketing and sales campaign.

DOCURATED

Docurated helps you create customized content for your prospects quickly and easily. This will allow you to locate specific keywords which relate directly to the individual or business which you are targeting, and then create relevant presentations for you based on those keywords. Your customers will see that you have put the time and effort into creating a presentation that is personal and unique specifically for them.

DATANYZE

This is a wonderful tool which will allow your sales representatives, or even yourself, the ability to track the customers that are buying from your competition, and more importantly, which customers have stopped buying from them. These customers would be other businesses that are within your target market, so if this tool tells you that a contract has just ended between them and your competitor, pick up the phone straight away and get them on board. Make sure that you find out why they left so that you can be sure that you do not make the same mistake.

TINDERBOX

TinderBox is perfect in the sales cycle when you are closing the sale. The tool will automatically create for you contracts, documents, emails, electronic signatures and so forth to make sure that the end of the sales cycle with your customers is as smooth and efficient as possible. The tool will also keep all of the information in your CRM software up-to-date, meaning that you will never be caught out giving your customers incorrect or out-dated information.

As you can see, the advance of technology has opened up the potential to allow businesses and individuals alike in the sales industry access to these tools which will revolutionize the way that they interact with customers. Put these tools in your hands or in the hands of your sales representatives, and watch your sales figures skyrocket.

Chapter 4 – How to Influence People

In order to be successful in sales, you must learn how to be a great leader. Anyone can be a leader, but true leadership comes from the deep innate ability or skill which allows you to influence people. If you look back through the pages of history, strong and influential people have ruled armies which had build dynasties and toppled kingdoms - although our sales business should not be managed to that extreme. The first step that you should take is to believe in yourself.

The biggest obstacle in doing this is that we as humans have the uncanny ability to constantly doubt ourselves. Thinking that we do not have what it takes to be the best that we want to be, we give in to fear and hinder our abilities before we even start. Realize that our biggest enemies are ourselves.

However, the most successful people that we see around us do not give in to this state of mind. They apply the five traits of successful people and overcome this silly obstacle, and then they are able to continue working on developing the skills required to influence people. The question is how do we influence people? When you think about it, it really comes down to leading by example – that kind of leadership that you share with your closest friends and family members. So, the question should rather be, how do you make more friends?

Making more friends definitely sounds better than the phrase "winning" more friends. So, how can this be achieved? What is it that we do that makes friends for us? It really comes down to five skills of which we should apply to every conversation that we have with people – sales prospects or strangers on the street.

1. Give your complete attention to someone else and show genuine interest in everything that they say to you.

2. Make sure that you do not forget their name (write it down if possible, or get a business card).

3. Listen to every word that they say.

4. Make the person feel important – that they are in the center of your attention.

5. Smile and thank them for their time.

When you think about it, isn't this the way that we act around our close friends and family members? This is how you should be acting around every person that you meet. Remember that the secret to a successful sales business is to build relationships to form long-term customers who will buy from you many times, so if we are able to master the art of relationship building, we should be able to turn every person that we meet into a loyal customer for life.

Chapter 5 – Sales Strategy

Just as the way as we are developing our decisions in the way that we interact and develop relationships with our customers, so too are they developing the way that they make decisions about how and why they purchase. These decision-making processes are constantly changing, so it is important to continually re-evaluate the way that you go about selling your products and services to your customers. You must also remember the difference between sales and marketing, and make sure that when you are selling, you do not come across as arrogant or as if you are not paying attention to what the customer has said in relation to what they actually need from you.

In essence, a sales strategy consists of a plan which positions a company's brand or product in order to gain a competitive advantage. The most successful types of sales strategies assist your sales team in focusing on target market customers and helping them communicate with them in helpful, relevant, and meaningful ways. Your sales representatives, and yourself, need to know how your products and/or services can be used to solve your customers problems. To be successful, your sales strategy should always be focused on presenting to the customers within your target market, else you will be wasting time trying to sell to customers who you have not tailored your products for.

In saying this, you should be well aware by now that in the sales business, your customer's needs should always come first. You should be asking as many relevant and quality questions as possible to make sure that what you are offering your customer is actually what they need. Sales is built on trust, and repeat business is the foundation of long-term success in the sales industry (or for any business for that matter), so lets have a look at six of the most effective steps that you can implement today to help you make sales and close the deal more efficiently.

IDENTIFY WHO MAKES THE BUYING DECISIONS

It is quite obvious when selling, that the only person who will buy or has the authority to buy, is the decision-maker. This especially applies when you are trying to win over a business as a new customer. You should always do your research first and try and understand how the decision-maker makes decisions, what motivates them to buy, and so on. Always customize and personalize your sales pitch so that you are specifically targeting that customer, and only that customer, at that time.

BE REALISTIC

When tailoring your sales pitch for the customer, make sure that you do not come across as too calculated, as this can actually scare some people off. In other words, show the customer that you care about identifying their needs and providing a solution to fix those needs rather than just making a quick sale. Remember that honesty and relationship-building are keys to success in the sales industry.

CREATE URGENCY

Your goal as a successful salesperson, is to get the customer to buy right now. You can't let your customer walk out of the door and say that they will be back next week, because they will either never come back, or they will buy from somebody else (you competition!). Whether you use your skills of persuasion by asking questions, or offer a discount if they purchase right now, or simply inform them that this price is only valid for today – when they come back next week, the product will be more expensive.

DEALING WITH OBJECTIONS

As discussed in Chapter Two, we need to ask for the sale in a way that if the customer is going to say no, that they are obligated to say more than no. Remember, ***"If I gave you the product at this low price, would there be any reason why you would not want to buy it today?"***. This sentence should be used at the end of every single one of your sales pitches. Not every customer, no matter how hard we try, is going to buy from us. But, we need to make sure that we understand and ask the reasons for them not buying with us. If we start to notice a pattern with customers who are not buying for similar reasons, we may need to change the way that we are dealing with things.

KNOW WHO YOUR COMPETITORS ARE

Running a business is tough. Consumers these days have so much choice and variety in product and price that you really need to stand out if they are going to buy from you. Look what your competition is doing, and then aim to constantly do better. You may not be able to always beat their prices, but you can definitely offer a higher quality of customer service than them – after all, sales businesses are built on relationships and repeat business.

BE PROFESSIONAL AT ALL TIMES

If your customer asks you a question that you don't know during your sales pitch, never make something up just to keep the pitch flowing. Tell your customer that you do not know, but you will find out the answer for them. You do not want to be caught out delivering false promises. Only talk about what you know, and maintain a high level of respect and professionalism with all of your customers at all times.

Chapter 6 – Cold Calling

Cold calling is the traditional practice of phoning unknown prospects in an attempt to establish business relationships with them. Whilst cold calling, you could be either selling your products or services, or simply setting up appointments with decision-makers who are responsible for making purchases. Over the years, cold callers, or telemarketers, have developed negative reputations and are considered to be nothing the sleazy salespeople who harass and intimidate people who do not want to buy, and the kind of salespeople who refuse to take no for an answer. However, cold calling is a legitimate form of marketing and is actually quite effective in developing long-lasting business and customer relationships just from a simple conversation over the phone.

WHAT DEFINES A COLD CALL

The definition of cold calling is simply the practice where a business or its sales representatives call potential customers to sell their products or services. It is called "cold" because the call is generally made without the prospects permission, and do not know the person calling them or the reason of the call. During the call, the sales representative will try and have a conversation with the prospect, normally from a script, in order to familiarize the customer with the business and its products.

WHAT MAKES A COLD CALL EFFECTIVE?

The effectiveness of a cold call is determined by a number of factors which will ultimately affect the outcome of the call. These factors include the personality of the sales representative (in this case, the telemarketer), how well they are able to use cold calling techniques, and how well they target the market which contains the prospects they would like as customers. Some studies have shown that you will close the deal, on average, 1 out of every 100 phone calls that you make, but this is not the attitude that you should have. Cold calling should not be considered a numbers game. If you look at it that way, out of every 100 customers that you call, 99 are going to be wasted, and only 1 will be worthwhile. You must consider **EVERY** call to be as important as the next, and you should be aiming to use all of the skills you have learned so far in this book in every call. There are successful telemarketers out there that have a success rate of up to 9 out of 10, so 90 sales out of every 100 phone calls. This should be your benchmark. Don't ever be discouraged however, just remember that every time that a customer says no, the next phone call could be a yes.

WHAT ARE SOME COLD CALLING TECHNIQUES?

Before you make a call, you should prepare, because in the telemarketing business, those who prepare will succeed. Not only should you know as much as possible about the products and services that you are selling, but you should also know everything about the brand or business that you are selling, who you target market is and why, and how you intend to actually go about having conversations with these prospects on the phone. The best technique when cold calling is to follow the sales strategy steps – ask the customer questions to identify their needs, listen to every word that the customer then says, asking for the sale and overcoming objections (the word "no"). Remember that you are trying to build relationships also, so if you put in the time and effort to reward your customer, your customer will reward you.

TOP TIPS OF SUCCESSFUL COLD CALLERS

You should be confident without coming across as cocky. This is achieved by making sure you listen to what the customer is saying and answer those questions without jumping in whilst they are talking to try and only close the deal as quick as possible. If you come across as genuinely confident, then it can be harder for customers to say no. People will listen to leaders and influential people, and this should go in par with your natural ability to be friendly and empathetic. Some of the most successful telemarketers and sales professionals say that when they pick up the phone, they smile whilst they are talking to the prospect or customer. This sounds silly since the customer cannot see you smiling through the phone, but believe it or not, you can hear people smiling through the phone – it comes across in the tone of your voice, and people will want to talk to people who are smiling.

You should also have a script which can guide you in your conversation on the phone. A script might be helpful when you first start out, but try and learn to have a conversation without it. Customers can hear if you are reading off of a script, because the conversation will become quite robotic and monotonous – and this will also give the customer the impression that it does not matter what they say to you, as you are not tailoring your answers to their problems to their specific needs, but rather only reading predetermined responses from a piece of paper.

On the note of research, although it may be near impossible to learn everything about a business or prospect before you call them (especially if you are calling individuals at their homes), you should still make sure that your research at least includes demographic research of your target market. For example, if you are selling your products or services to people who love skateboards, then research as much as you can about those people – what type of skateboards do they like, what brands do they prefer, what major factors will affect the type of skateboards that they purchase.

This rule can be applied to any target market. When you are having a conversation with a prospect over the phone, showing them that you are knowledgeable about the products that they love, then it will be much easier to develop relationships with them. It also helps you if they ask you a question about products in that market – you will have done your research so you should be able to answer them.

Most importantly however, you should be keeping good records of your calls and be taking notes from every call. Implement one of the sales tools that we looked at in a previous chapter to keep these records. That way, you will have a detailed list of people who you have called, have not called, objections, reasons for not buying, appointment times for call backs, and so on. You should also consider having a diary to keep a good record of dates and times that customers have requested you to call them back if they needed you to get more information or did not have the time to talk to you when you first called.

Conclusion

In summary, by reading this book you should now have the required basic skills to succeed in the sales industry. We have learned that sales is a personalized process which differs from marketing, and that successful salespeople share five traits – discipline, tenacity, implementation, focus, and desire. We have also learned that when we ask for the sale, we should be asking a question which makes the customer give a reason for why they are not going to buy today. This way, you can explore with the customer ways that you can overcome this objection.

This book has also shown you the various sales tools and sales strategies which will allow you to effectively develop your business into a very successful organization, and the key to this development is built upon developing long-lasting relationships with our customers by asking quality and relevant questions. Lastly, we looked at some simple cold calling techniques which you can use to increase your sales conversion rate when making phone calls to potential customers.

Use this book as a guide and reference on your journey to becoming a successful salesperson, and always remember that it is up to us to make the decision to be successful. Come back and read this book any time that you need to refresh your skills or need motivation or inspiration, as this book will surely help you succeed.

Thank you for reading. I hope you enjoy it. I ask you to leave your honest feedback.

47811304R00027

Made in the USA
San Bernardino, CA
08 April 2017